AF261160

POSTCARDS FROM MEXICO

POSTCARDS FROM MEXICO

Poems

JAMIE ROSS

SUNSTONE PRESS

SANTA FE

© 2022 by Jamie Ross
All Rights Reserved
No part of this book may be reproduced in any form or by any electronic or mechanical means including
information storage and retrieval systems without permission in writing from the publisher,
except by a reviewer who may quote brief passages in a review.

Sunstone books may be purchased for educational, business, or sales promotional use.
For information please write: Special Markets Department, Sunstone Press,
P.O. Box 2321, Santa Fe, New Mexico 87504-2321.
Printed on acid-free paper

Library of Congress Cataloging-in-Publication Data

Names: Ross, Jamie, 1946- author.
Title: Postcards from Mexico : poems / by Jamie Ross.
Description: Santa Fe, NM : Sunstone Press, [2022] | Summary: "A collection
    of poems in tandem with the images that inspired them, postcard photos
    from indigenous Mexico by a group of nine photographers"--provided by
    publisher.
Identifiers: LCCN 2022019549 | ISBN 9781632933690 (paperback)
Subjects: LCGFT: Poetry.
Classification: LCC PS3618.O84527 P67 2022 | DDC 811/.6--dc23/eng/20220520
LC record available at https://lccn.loc.gov/2022019549

WWW.SUNSTONEPRESS.COM
SUNSTONE PRESS / POST OFFICE BOX 2321 / SANTA FE, NM 87504-2321 /USA
(505) 988-4418 / FAX (505) 988-1025

FOR OUR FAMILY, EVERYWHERE.

PHOTOGRAPHS BY

Jonathan Amith
Ruth Lechuga
Micaela McGuirk
Walter Reuter
José Ángel Rodríguez
Clare Brett Smith
Antonio Turok
Mark Turok
Mariana Yampolsky

CONTENTS

CONTENTS
(CONTINUED)

PRELUDE

In the late 1990s, Jamie Ross, the poet and painter who imagined this book into existence, ventured from his life in bilingual, bicultural northern New Mexico to a new adventure in Mexico. The result is this magical multi-voiced, multi-pictured collection: a group of remarkable photos from a group of remarkable photographers, combined with Ross's enchanting and extraordinary poems.

One of this reader's delightful first discoveries was that the "Postcards from Mexico," the pictures in the book, were indeed actual postcards, brilliant black & white photographs by nine artists, illuminating the life of the country's indigenous people.

By 1997, at his home near Taos, New Mexico, Ross was already combining his paintings with poetry. That fall, at a gallery show in Santa Fe, he met Leovigildo Martínez, an artist from Oaxaca. Leo was also wedding texts with his pictures. "Come to Mexico," Leo urged. "You—and your art—will be embraced."

The following spring, Ross arrived in Oaxaca to paint. He never set up his easel. From his first day, in the city's mercados, galerías and museum shops, he discovered a series of astonishing photo cards—striking images of people in regions like Chiapas, Guerrero, Michoacán—that would become the core of this book.

Captivated, Jamie spent his time writing poems and stories on these *postales*, sending them to friends, family in New Mexico. Within weeks, the postcards themselves began to *speak*—their own poems in their own voice. They were *calling;* he had to find more of these images, their families, their places, their songs.

And soon, too, he had to find the photographers. So began a journey that would take buses, taxis, backroads, carts, inns and years. He once described, in a short essay, what he experienced and observed along the way:

The highways that transect the cities, the autopistas and tourist routes are clean, direct, maintained. The government sees to that. But take a trip into Mexico's deep remote body. Take a second-class bus, let's say, from Oaxaca to Huautla, or from Hujuapan de León to Santiago Juxtlahuaca. The interior roads are twisted, narrow and pitched, the pavement split.

Along each side cacti, thorn trees converge or soar, broken and refulgent, pinned with foil, plastic bags, punctured dolls, bloodied towels, chicken necks and crosses. Beyond are fields, carved from want and stone; a distant man slowly walking behind a plow, a gray, white-faced donkey.

Nothing here is flat. All is steep, spectacular, ascending or down, cliff, mountain, desert, jungle. Suddenly, around any turn: three men playing tubas, drinking pulque; a burro roped in flagstone; a table stacked with oranges, mangos, broiled chicharón, candied roosters covered with flies.

The toilets don't work on a second-class bus. You bring your food, or you wait—and stow your geese, baby goats, bundles of cane, bagged salt, a favorite hen or paralyzed dog—all in the doors below. At every village, a young girl or wizened man clambers into the aisle, with cardboard trays of peanuts, melon cubes, cinnamon cones, roasted corn on a stick.

And the wrappers, the cobs and wooden skewers—from every finger-smeared open window—fly out into the night or rising sun, into mesquite trees, rosary beads, speared tin cans; and the screech of the bus as it careens another embankment. And plunges deeper, into the stories, the people and music awaiting you ahead.

Whatever bus or road you're taking, whatever bird or rabbit you're carrying, whatever trail you may be plowing, welcome to these pages. May your journey here be marvelous.

—F. Harlan Flint

POSTCARDS FROM MEXICO

Una Mirada al Futuro, Jonathan D. Amith

POMEGRANATE

First it was blank. I sat down
in the cross-caned chair. Took out
the box from the missionaries. Opened
the lid to the jars of paint. Here
was my brush, with the panther's
hair. And the blackthorn branch
it leapt from. Three dogs,
writhing on the ground, one-armed
Carlos, propped against a stump,
putting in the bullet. I opened
the black. The moon went out, the
parrots went dun. I heard
a girl scream, then low-voice, sing
for Rosarita. I found the song:
gold, and blood. Gardenias. And
the gourds spun in their autumn
fire, and wept beneath
the table. Ocaño's pigs broke
a wall, trampled the beans, the
new-picked maíz, rolled the ears
on the hard-packed floor. I heard
the dirt. I smelled your groin. I
opened the tangerine. The sun
rose on Ameyáltepec. I lifted
the baby into my lap. The women
left the comal, moved their sewing
onto the terrace. So, do they tend
the world. I saw you in the ochre
fields, bent behind the mule. I
opened the ditch. The donkey
brayed. Six grapefruit dropped
from a tree. A mango cracked. I
opened the red. I made two lines
for my lips. Two more, curved,
for yours. *When will the future
kiss me again?* The planets, silent,
circled the sun. The gourds
turned in their sleep. I combed
my hair. Lifted the baby to my
breast. I loosened my blouse. I
opened the blue.

PART ONE

CELEBRACIÓN DE LA CARRETERA

Because you see my daughter and she is sound.
Because I bought this chair this tiny chair
for thirty pesos, took it from the luggage rack
behind the plaza, the basilica. How I sit so
wide like this, my big sombrero green-spread
wings. Because the celebration for the road, today
is for the road. Because the ribbons all the girls
will cross the street and back again, a thrill
of ribbons, and the band from Las Colimas, priests
and dignatarios, speeches, black micrófonos. Because
it is the old way with the stones before the time
of Vasco. And before the furniture. Because it breathes
the babies and tamales, the carts of yellow chickens
mangos rolling on the stone, the street is empty
and the woman rising. Because we sit like this. The hummingbirds.

Ermitas de Oxchuc, Antonio Turok

IT WAS ONLY BY CHANCE

that the air could speak. I knew the ground
by your feet upon it. I knew a ceiling, but not
a room. It was only by chance the shape of
an echo.

It was only by chance a bus. Some would say
a bird. Others say a weasel—Even now I pinch
my tongue to say it was no dream. To say
it was your room. To say *in all directions*
it was a bus—I drew it with a map
I had the paints— you know I brought them
Even now I pinch
this chance to move a wall, to move this shape
I swear, I drew it
moving from a church, moving in the palms, moving
from your lips
        to my toes—
           I swear it was a bus.

El Trompetista, José Ángel Rodríguez

EL TROMPETISTA

Without him there is no Oaxaca—
and I'm a foot, an inch, away.
No one tunes him down.
I'm in a bar, turning up the violins,
drowning in a *cantadora*.
Outside on the street
oxen are stampeding, buses
honking, cars blue with oil, mufflers
dragging by wires.
Engines never idle here. Transport
is only an excuse for percussion.
In the beginning was the word.
In the beginning was the noise.
In the beginning, this man
plays the biggest trumpet ever made.
And I'm only a foot, an inch,
a scream away.

Selva Lacandona, Micaela McGuirk

IPENEMA

I couldn't sleep.
The band from Ipenema
is playing next door.
I have the book—
You won't believe the pictures.
Leave the stretchers in the car.
Leave the car in Colorado.
I have the ink.
I have the stamps—

Jesus, child, you have the blood.

Meet me in Ipenema.
They're playing
next door.

La Alfarera, Clare Brett Smith

WOMAN WITH POTS

Some of them break.
The mud can be bad to begin with.
Last week the horse
fell on its way to market—
Three months of heartbeat
coiled in a road.
My lungs say the air is bad. And
I cannot see the mountains:
the view is choked by dirt.
But in the street there is a map—
not within the bricks, I'd say
but between them, where the moisture is.
The skin of snakes marks this clay.
The horse was not stupid.
We do what we feel,
not what we are taught.

Maternidad, Antonio Turok

We're looking out front. The message

we know, will come from there. Open
like a future, a surprise, prophecy
delivered—a letter in a bottle. Open

like men, beneficent. Perhaps
even ugly. But beautiful, in the way
we know ostriches, moles, monkeys; say

monkey-like, but winged, medieval—with
torch-flame tails, comet's, or candle-ray. Or

none at all. Men
like that. Lighting in a field, just outside
the barn. What they'd call a barn. Though

we call a hutch. Rabbits

have no fear then—isn't
this strange?—After sunset, every
highway, any road, they

play the headlights, the sound
of a car, dash across the bumper, before

you can brake. Always
we're looking. I brake a lot. Sometimes
I hit them. Things

land at night. In the dark. Often
in the past.

La Sombra, José Ángel Rodríguez

LA SOMBRA

The way they said it,
we weren't sure—
The sky was that open?
A bird a stream?
The way they pointed and exhaled,
turned their skin
around, around, so wet
around itself—The way the moon
went in the sun—Who
could walk away? Keep fingers
from our mouths?
No one needed maps
or writing in a book—
It was so new, so old, at once.
The melons were rotten, the silver black—
we saw that:
A bent man crouched in a field for life.
But the grain that flowed from the woman
all red and thick with guava—
we saw that too.
The sun fell in the ocean.
We didn't flinch.
How can you be sure,
if you can't move?
How could you move
if you were sure?

Amusgos, Ruth D. Lechuga

TRIANGLE

I never smoked until today—
Not until the dog came.
One, two, three. That was us.
Then the dog came, in from the edge.
Not a whole dog, mind you,
but the front of something,
like a train from Guatemala
or weather moving through.
We've never seen its tail.
We've never seen the full dog.
One, two, three. We keep counting.
I roll tobacco.
Without smoke,
nothing would appear.

El Cañaveral, José Ángel Rodríguez

EL CAÑAVERAL

When you get this card
you'll be combing your hair
like you always do. You'll be standing
in flowering corn—like you always are.
You'll be walking in your chocolate shoes,
watering the green part. Watering the
No tire basuras en la carretera, watering
the buses. Watering the diesel
in a man
who wants you in this restaurant, its
doors *flung* open—Wants you
in this poem, its dirty napkins
on the table, its fallen silver, empty
bowls of *mole, camarones*—Wants you
in the creases of these walls, these broken
chairs, broken bricks, broken-Spanish fingers
writing one word at a time

you'll be combing your hair
you'll be combing your hair
you'll be combing your hair

PART TWO

EL CERVANTINO

The poet came to dinner yesterday

With his children, he said.

And he sat down
between three empty chairs.

To his right—Edna, he said.
There, to his left: Cristál. Next
over, finally, Robin.

And he did not ask much food. Only,

Edna would like salad. Cristál,
her passion is the bird, the darkest juices;

And Robin—his love is roots, you know:
potatoes, *jícama*, carrots—
and the rabbit lying with them.

The plates, themselves, not large
but each handmade, Saltillo. Ordered
by our host, Jiménez,
for just this fall occasion

When all the farmers and their wives,
the dancers, entertainers
would join the miners and officials
who'd brought the train, the silver, all
the candles, *carga, cargadores.*

Thanks to God, Jiménez said—*A Dios!*
Gracias for this feast! And so he raised his glass.

And then we saw the children—
Edna, Robin, and Cristál

Their plates wiped clear as windows.

La Semilla, Antonio Turok

Sometimes I feel as if
I'm chasing an endless tail
on an endless dog. But then

I think of the milk-pod seed, and
my daughter blows me a kiss.
Is she my daughter? Is she
my hope? She's

Just a photograph. And I—
like this. Every time I open
my question, she's
there: Her lips

Pursed to the camera, where
mine might be—air, wing, a
butterfly. A man, outstretched,

About to be blown

Apart.

Selva Lacandona, Micaela McGuirk

HERON

When you don't speak, I can't fly—
Trees cut. Sky torn. Streams
rammed in a pail. My breath
crammed in a bucket, on
a woman's head.
All I hear is logs.
Fish in the water mimic me:
fins, big mouth, no sound.
All I hear is logs. All I feel
is life in a bucket, groping
for lines in a swim of cranes, fishing
for weave in a bird's bolt, craning
metal, bent around its welds, sides
bulged, hollow sunk, dumb
thunk against a wall. All I see
is one mute hole
where the handle fit, where
a girl once grasped her heart
and stretched beyond her skin—
streaming with trout. Screaming
for trees. Trees
so tall they touched the clouds.

Eclipse, Antonio Turok

GREYFALL

La Herradura was our ranch before the
greyfall. A strange term for something

made of birds. Our girls, five and nine,
were dancing on the wide stone fence, ballet

shoes we'd found in town. The car
was rough; I'd guessed the carburetor, maybe

points if we were lucky. Then, I thought:
the fuel pump. On my back, beneath the Ford.

The baby Jesus! He—gasped Edna—He
was all…just

feathers!

Selva Lacandona, Micaela McGuirk

LAME HORSE

I don't know how
to say "lame horse"
in Spanish. Or the language of
your legs, their trembling

As you write in silence,
staring at a window.

How time
sings to our ankles, gives
us wings. So often
takes them back.

What the words are
one foot crosses.
Then the other
that is gone.

LAS VARAS

It was not like that—not for days the
hard as fire driven under snow, the

round the wheel an elsewhere, a blue
lost in all blue, your eyes

not like that, the buses held, they *held*—I can

show you water where the children—*all* the children
pushed the windows, struck the trees, cactus, the garbage-

painted mountains, the movie in the TVs *moving upside-
down*—a girl's frog *a girl's frog* twitching like your

lips, *upside-down*—not like *held a promise—A promise!*—they
held glass, screens, a man's dog *a man's dog*—your words *pinned*

yelping *upside-down*—Show you where the women—*the women*
bent the metal seats, baby-studded fabric cracked

cement, the wretched buildings, palms—*for your hands*
the skewed one, open-mouthed, pulled dark braid, *pulled*

the goat—*grabbed it—head out from the crate, splattered*
dam still slick around it, held it *held it in you* creased wet hot split

only sky beneath me—

LA DISTROFIA

The sky receives its letters
with less attention now. Her first meanings

were *owls*. The nests
of straw-like integers, lying

in this plowing motion.
Burro is less

than what she calls her drawing—
A dragging animal, larger

than a crayon's hand, under pins,
a haystack. The way the heart's

squared-off sides
join to form its scrutiny, inner

stable, lined with family *we*. My own
darkness asks your envelope, all the silver

star-gears, breakness, osteopic box, face
of all the presidents, mottled

with no consonants, seven knots of
rub me please—The mule, *It's got a baseball!*—All

our open days again—Veracruz, the rain the boys the crowd
the scribbled dogs, the man beyond the fence—

The *rain*, its blue—*Look, so blue!*—
becomes itself that easily.

Vendedora de Carne, Antonio Turok

VENDEDORA DE CARNE

You ask me for the God of Meat. Not

On this counter. Not in this stall. Here
tripe, hocks, chorizo, a scrawny goose
with the feet attached. I like
the feet attached. Always have. Though
others in this business usually chop

Them off. They get more for the bird
like that—auto parts versus the car. Piece
by piece: replace the body and suspension,
vinyl seats, rubber seals. There's money

In it two ways—Fix the hair, the heart
falls out (let's say, if you were human)—
Paint your lips, you step in mud.
I should be selling boots. Where
there's mud, there's hunger. Go down

To the slaughterhouse, up above the Rio.
Watch what spews out from the drain
and floats into the water. You ask me
how to find the God. I always leave
the webs for that.

Zinacantán, Antonio Turok

TWO GIRLS GUARDING A TABLE

We keep the babies in here.
In our secret room.
You see cups and pots, stacked
in a jumble. That's our way
of fooling you. You see an easel,
drips of paint. A woman calls
from the cliffs of Crete. That's
our way of fooling you.
The highways are open. Our
room is not. The buses
run to Mérida, Mitla—they run
to Taxco's silver. You might
take one anywhere—for
the liquid in the pots, the
broad curve of a brush. For the arc
within this woman's voice. That's
our way of fooling you. You
might circle the world:
You won't see our babies.

El Ixcán, Antonio Turok

THE SHAMAN'S WIFE, WITH BIRDS

Because you lost, you left
these three: I embrace them. They
were not your enemies. Even now
I cry for them, not

for you—while they sing, talk
happily, much like our old days. I
cannot stop this crying. It grows like
children grow, jumping rope, rope

spun into braid, bone, hair thick as the
road I wear. The buses run all night—they,
like you, cannot stop. The aisles, like you
are filled with clatter, rumbling, ceaseless

voices—with each empty seat, a speaker
overhead. The tickets are cheap. Your
cost was high. The women from the buses:
These were not my friends. The moan

of them around you: This was not
my dream. I dreamt bells, that clear—
a man, our child, a home. The hills
that ring Pátzcuaro, skipping

from the ground. Feel
this gravel dress—I tie it, harsh, for
memory. How you drove inside. While
these three were under you. Now

you run. At least, they fly.

PART THREE

THE CURANDERA AND HER SON

Edgar! and *Guillermina!*
That's how the parrot says their names.
That's how the parrot will say yours too,
orange and blue and red

When you sit on the rough-hewn bench
in the dark room, on the dirt floor
littered with stems and leaves, littered
with bundles of *hierbas, raíces!*—

That's how the parrot says it

While you wait with the man
with the blisters, the nun
who can't stop sighing, the girl
with one green, deep green eye, staring

At this parrot,
hanging
            upside-down,
by one yellow leg
from a tin trapeze
Swinging slowly, back and forth

Cooing *Guillermina Jesus Jesus*
squawking *Dios! Edgar! Dios!* whistling *Alma Mía! Doña Ana!*
pleading *Fela, Fabi, Tito,* shrieking *Madre! Sangre! Santa
Reyna!* laughing *Pancho O Pancho!* giggling, scratching, gurgling *Rosa!*
spitting *Alfredo!* spewing *Moises!* swooning *Flora,* scraping *blue,* slicing
orange, splicing *gold,* stitching, pleating, weeping

María. Weeping

María.

Staring

Green—*Deep* green

From a tin trapeze.

Al Río Jatate, José Ángel Rodríguez

AL RÍO JATATÉ

First it was me, with the pail. And
I went to the stream, looked in the water:

Voilá!—Another woman
with a bucket on her head!—Just

like mine. Just like me. On Tuesday
we went back, together like this, to gather

from the river. And…Just like that!—Two *more!*—
each like me. Each in a bucket, with *her* bucket!

Now, in just two days: *Four of us!*—Each
with a bucket, a woman in each bucket, each

one with a bucket on her head.
As above, so below. All

the men can do is drink.

Echando Redes, José Ángel Rodríguez

THE NET

All's not what you see. Here I am, the
river: a man, throwing the world. How
I love to throw your world! So, so much string
spins above the other—the other side, the
stream, the wet side turning. And I wade
into that side: flume of fish, murk, mud
beneath my feet, sliding from arroyos, the
TV in the kitchen—it's baseball from New
York! The Cuban kid is batting. And the birds
shoot from the cages, high! High above
the distant mesas climbing in their ribs, high
above María. High above Miami where
I play the conga in the salsa and the world
swirls her flamenco. High above the fans
where she is weaving through the tables with
her silver hands a slender thread that jets
across two buildings, over rocks, above the
stars. I throw them all. One is yours. The other
mine. The spraying air, *hear the cheers!* Your
body spins above me, singing. How one holds
the other! I wade into the current, deeper. And
throw. Throw. I throw!

Selva Lacandona, Micaela McGuirk

SHOES

All night the boats
drift through the jungle, long
shoes. My shoes, the elephants', our
elemental hollow *would*. The
burned-out log the will

creates. Does it float, does it
hold you? The vines
twist: *No answer. But*
elephants remember. Ask
them to appear—
                    Hah!—Since

when do *they* need to! You

can't see their little chairs. Or
their linking trunks, pencil tails
in the Chinese watercolor. A
hidden falls—wide brush. The river
draws the river. What else
did you expect? You stroke
them with your hands. They walk
you on the water.

Pato al Horno, José Ángel Rodríguez

So good to be a turkey, outside
our house. Hot in the house. Shrinks
you like shrink wrap. Remember

The heads they sell from the Pacific?
In our little *casa,* we can do them too.
Such a fine turkey, even this small.

When it was you—
Now *there* was a problem.

CAMALEÓN

I see it in his hands. In the stone
he works with a silent knife.
His year-old son
twists in a hammock. His Huichol wife
smokes, at her weaving.
I see it in the brook
threading by your rambled house. The way
you've moved the lilac, cleared
the *epazote*. Two pale sheets, hung
across a line. I see

It's not the bleeding. The canyon
holds no light. For all
that you might carve it. The canyon
holds no light. The soul's
not one
who cannot call, tangles the cord
in a lantern dream. The shape
is not Hornillos,
a pulp mill in a basin.
The seamstress told you truths.
But she could not pull the strings apart.

EVA'S SONG

You're a mason, he said to nothing
but a wall, and no one saw the wall
deny it. No one saw a verb, but
the sun spoke, and Eva's children

Sang the song. Her small house
built of string, strips of foil from
a wastebasket, pasted on a story
that desire had told her. *Early loss*

Is green, is all the days beginning
it would say, before the ground
found her, in the pale start of dawn.
Even then, cold waves held her naked,

Hooked like a fish. The trowels on
tables left by workmen, too tired
to finish what one could never start: Eva's
song of castles, olives, a duke from Cadiz

Who had given gloves, a pendant, decked
her trees with silver lights—but took away
her breath, her fin-like feel for water. Now
a single emerald shape

Floated, silent—the first shadows
of a dark month, a black year, her moon's
distant fingers clinging to a tinseled wall;
her daughters' easy voices

Piling the ceaseless snow.

Ollas, Mariana Yampolsky (Courtesy Fundación Mariana Yampolsky)

1001 NIGHTS

1001 genies. Where
did they go? What happened
To the wishes? The body

tricks you every time. All
I asked, one him to the next, was
just three words: To be free. All

I've got's a lot, dirt unto dirt
piled with pots—barreled, squat,
vats, crocks: stacks, walls,

blocks of pots. Horizons
of pots, constant sighing—
Rub Me, Rub Me. See

my sign?: Lorena, Queen
Of Tureens. Hung in the shrine
where the cross would be. Some

people say I got my wish: "At least,
now, they're empty." *Rub Me, Rib
Me, Rob Me, Robe Me.* Your voice

gets ruder and lewder.

Las Hermanas Galán, Clare Brett Smith

STRUT YOUR STUFF

Wow! The best one we've made yet—*And*
our first with feathers. The feathers
take a steady hand. You have to be strong
to do this. The dancing steps! The *dancing*
steps: Our secret. Two strong sisters *know*
their secrets. We're calling it George. George
Washington. For the wig, of course. And
yes: the Bill. *Valuable.* Our declaration
of independence. And it's our first with
features. Ugly? Hey, we're young. It's hard
to find a man out here. Mostly sinew
like their steers, pigs: *gristle.* Hard. Hard
to tell them apart. It's *Ugly?* Hey, we'll grow. At
least this one is useful. No more grubs. No
more weevils—What's your beef? All
day we sit turning pots: bowls for the *plancha,*
cazuelas for the oven—Hey! George! Strut
Your Stuff!—*Now*
          There's something to eat!

Celia, Antonio Turok

CELIA

"— is a very good little girl. She combs her
own hair and washes her hands. Mamá has
dressed her in a blue bow. It is very bright."
—Inscription on a blackboard, Chiapas

I'm going to write about Celia now. The
Truth. Me,
Celia. I'm going to do it here, on
                              This part
Of the statement board: the side of
                  Mathematics. Underneath
Those columns of equations—
            Less than < , More than >,
                  Equals =. To write it
Like it should be: Frank
Arithmetic. A summary, the Truth, right
                  Below the line. I've waited
Short enough—*bows, combs, hair.* Cute:
You
Up there, me down here. Now
I'm going to tell you. From the floor, into
The blank above—
                  Black!: An open night
About to burst with stars. See, here, my wand—

No One Reckons With Celia

BURROS OUTSIDE SAN YSIDRO

A swerve. A slot. A bad one. Who knew
what they were doing here, never would be safe—
A broken zone. Freak scene—Burros
on the highway, in the darkness, blocked
sharp, slapped, in air, rearing, one

Against four others, two more in
the headlights ghastly, screaming, open
gashes split by hooves, teeth, kicks, punches—
spitting, shrieking, matted mud-clot bloody

Burros, taken, the way men who labor
then are beaten, men who
work the factories, the stock forks, men
who heave the canisters, transmissions,
men who wrench trucks, muck sewage, whip
their laden carriers, men whipped, men

Taken in a bar, sudden and explosive
after too much whiskey, too much nothing,
taking out the tables, taking
out the chairs, arms, legs, taking off
the backs, walls, fixtures, doors, men

Taking out each other
in an alley, on the street, gravel, rut,
bone by bone, sister, mother, scraps
of paper, braided rope, grease-pit
asphalt, rock, brick, glass, stars, a
promise—when no one else but they

Are left to fight it out.

NUESTRA SEÑORA DE LA SOLEDAD

*In the Purépecha church at Tzintzúntzan, Michoacan, a glass casket
rests on the altar, containing a quilt-wrapped sculpture— the body
of the Interred Christ. Each year the swaddling linens are changed.
Each year the sculpture is discovered to have increased in length..*

Longer, so much longer growing
now I cannot hold him. The snow
is white the sheets I hold this white
but he is bloody. Not my blood I swear
the sheets before me his—I wrapped
him yes but large too large we
need more space the flesh his
skin this waxen, scratched and pale the
hanging animal so hard it is
so hard to fit to cover it the body he
said eat my body, only I
can know his head beyond
the bed the closet
auricle the pumping
vein of us this glassy box I see
through it my own transfigured
glassed-in face—I cut
the box before the bed, the stuffing
mattress swollen I
am only flesh I say
this on my spreading knees my
spreading prayer I swear the way
of my own hair it grows too large the
God of it the sin I wash no sin but
that of rags his rib this altar-womb
I cannot cross or come
with him.

San Andres de Larrainzar, Antonio Turok

LA ANUNCIACIÓN

First I put on the horse. Then
I put on the legs, the two
bare feet. Next, I put on

The earth. And I walked
for you. I walked you
to Granada. After that

To Bethlehem. First I
followed the star. O!, I thought.
I turned at the light. I found

The gray bus from Osingo. I
took it into Chilón—to Lipan's
Abarrotes. Calle Limones,

Number twenty-two. Two men
were standing outside, smoking
cigarettes. I took off my hat. They

Disappeared. Lipan
was at the counter. Lipan, I
said, I need a broom. The horse

Forgot its tail. I see, he said
I have one cheap. Now

We could ride to December.

PART FOUR

VIEW OF GUANAJUATO

We're shown the tunnels. Vaulted churches. The statue
of a hero, spotlit above the city, fist raised to a flame.

But you don't see the lovers, huddled horizontal, those
wrought-iron benches strewn around the plaza, slathered
with the palest, thickest plastic paint—the boy, his

Whisper-cradle hands

Don't see the dogs, shadowing a cow
too weak to truck, too thin for market
who holds her calf against a wall, can't

See the woman, shawled, sprawled on the sidewalk, groping
for some scattered branches; one peso a bundle, a day's cut
of saplings—each leaf, dangling, silver as a breath—

Or the collared bear, dumb with pain, hanging by a chain

Over six staring children. A blue ball in a gutter. A fruit stand—
pineapple in wheels, all around the glass. Glasses

Filled with melon
so green it could be candy

Or Tony Griego's first planting,
just above Las Tablas,
just broken through the earth.

It could be broken with a sigh, the earth is so easy.

Feel the girl arch her back, eyes squeezed tight, lips apart,
her arms wrapped in a circle—

Just like pineapple. It's that easy.

Papaloteando, José Ángel Rodríguez

CEREMONIA DE LA COMETA

Come, let's take down the book. And open
to the children

Who stream across a rough-grown field
deep in reeds and silk-flower, grasses
thick with celebration; children

Flying kites. The simple kind,
made by hand at school. Each one
unpainted, new: a skin-light diamond,
waiting for its test, a string tied to two struts
on the eve of Easter.

Not much wind. So they run, these kids;
they're running like a flock of deer, like
streaking birds, running to create it—their
breath for its breath—the paper body's

Open star, stretched upon a cross,
children pulling, squealing, shouting. Some

Stumble. Have fallen in the weeds
and phlox. Others—knees high, legs
pumping, call to nearby hills and houses:
"Watch me, everybody! Watch us!"

While some are simply gliding, fixed
upon the upper air
as blue as it can mean. No one's
looking back. And all of them are laughing

In this meadow cut from mountains, jungle,
stone and human labor. Just out
from their last class, trying with all they've
got. Tugging on this one thin string

Just before ascension.

Mujer Sembrada, José Ángel Rodríguez

MUJER SEMBRADA

What was I growing?
You know.
Sticks? Cactus?
I planted turtles in their husks,
gave them cane to breathe.
What grows is my belly
and you within it.

My eyes
see you outside—you,
with your hips
as round as the sun. But
the earth says otherwise—
As much as I would bathe in light,
your dark skin bathes in mine.

What was I growing?
A crop without shells.
A fence that will fall down.
As naked as your breath
I sow my seed for you.

Fiesta de San Sebastían, Antonio Turok

FIESTA DE SAN SEBASTIÁN

No one cries today! Not the thronging streets, the
trumpets, tuba, floats, the wool salesmen, not
these *flowers*—We were born for flowers! And
the dancers' tambourines my sisters Mamá
her lifting lilac dress, your crystal body
pierced by arrows, shoots
of brilliant springtime passion
blooming white gardenia as you pass
above us—Horse of nature spraying petals: *Scent
can make me crazy!* Brightly burning here I
flame to melt your mystery, blood of lilies virgin
grotto bleating goats new lambs electric
big Dos Equis. Past the church, banana trees, the
tissue tearing leaf by leaf, rose by rose the
trucks so high I hardly hear the swooping birds, the
engines underneath the platform croon for this we now
have risen. See! I hold this bowl for you, my open
fragrant gourd half-painted deep geranium. And too
my sisters, iris, vases, waiting, while the grandmas
tap the pavement with their wooden stems and
crutches. All flowers bare their secret to you
throbbing wheels and drumbeats, pungent
through the village—All of us one blossom, one
single aching question: *When*—
When will you rain!

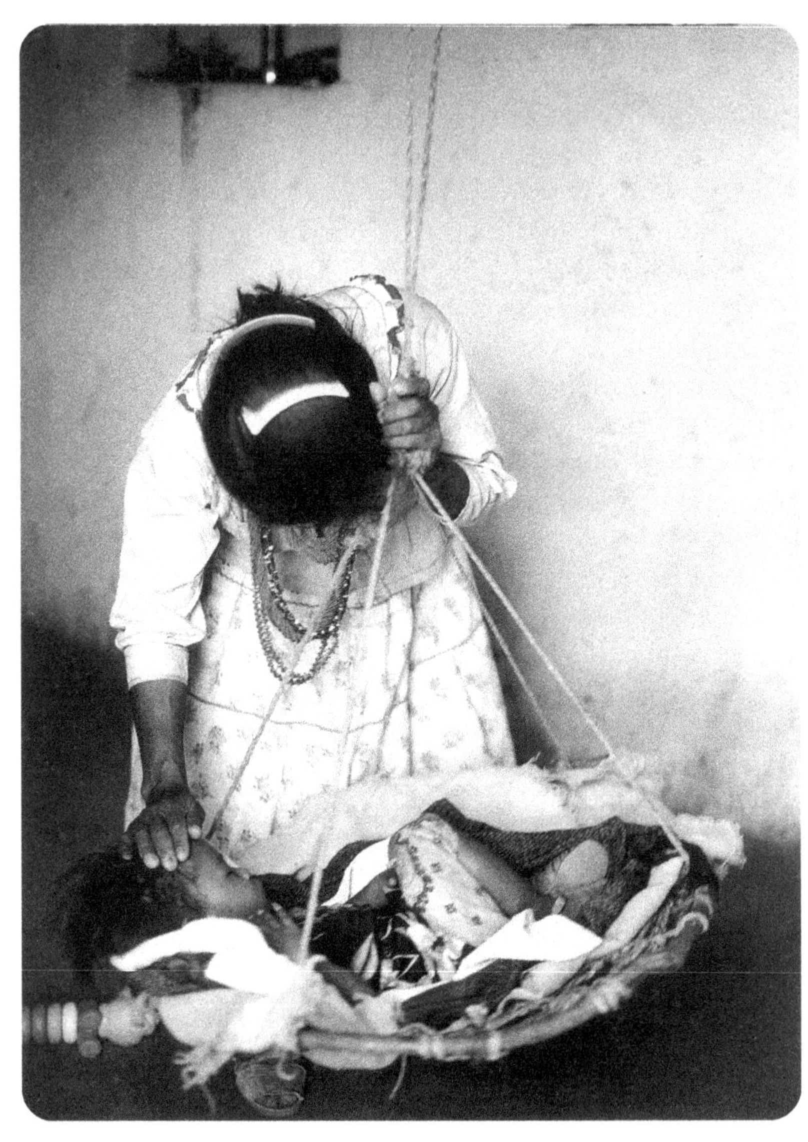

Arrullo, José Ángel Rodríguez

I WEIGHED MY LIFE

It was not my life that fell
(as if the beam had shattered free)
but the overwhelming gifts—
nuts, pillows, tangerines,
your hand upon my face—
that brought us earthward,
left the balance

weightless

Músicos, Mariana Yampolsky (*Courtesy Fundación Mariana Yampolsky)*

WHEN MOZART PLAYS IN OCOTLÁN

I drink with the blind man and his daughter—
Who fills his glass, holds his basket.
An earthen hut. A slab of mud.
Three cows so haunched and gray
They disappear
            In the dark of insects.
            In the basket of insects
Where he gropes
For roasted wings and brittle heads—squeezes
The shelled bodies, salted legs, singing softly
   Chapulínes!
            Cóme! Cóme!
                  Then pulls out
            A blackened thorax—shouts
                  Chapulínes! Chapulínes!—
                  Flings his arms above his head,
                  Pumps them up and down
                  Chapulínes! Saltár! Saltár!
                  Like bows of violins—

His daughter grabs his legs
                  Up and down—
Her hair in a ribbon
                  Up and down—
                  Saltár! Saltár!
A scarlet bow
                  Up and down—

She feeds the cows,
Boils the *sopa*
                  Up and down—
Builds the fire for
      Chapulínes!
Steers his hand
Back to his glass of
                  Violins, violas,
                  Cellos, bassos, *concertinas*
                  Up and down—
                  Saltár! Saltár!
As bright as a *fiesta,*
            As red and deep as Moonblood—

            When Mozart plays in Ocotlán.

Vista Típica Mexicana, Mark Turok

THE DRESS

Sometimes the buses ask the fields, passing
Field after field. The question, always, for

The donkey. Not the man in his grey hat, the
River far beyond. Or the ghosting ocotillo, walled

Against the highway; clung with paper, plastic
Bags. Headlamps, sliding into snow. You, then

Wide. And falling. Now, only white. The dress,
What happened to the dress? The windows open

Curious rows of water, one face

Floating on the dirt. Above the wheels, the
Satellites sit watching from their seats. I still

Hold the package. Gold string, and bows
Shooting through the night. Donkey in a furrow

Drinking its own other. Moon, moon, lip
To lip. Naked donkey. Drinking. Naked.

Tell Me.

Volcán de Santiaguito, Antonio Turok

LAST SUPPER

It took months to prepare.
Tilling bare rock
was hard enough.
The wind tore seed
we'd yet to sow.
We prayed for rain—
El Dios didn't screw around.
Sharks ate our sheep.
Then the sun
burned craters in our valleys.

But no one took our *salsa.*
And no one
stole our stones.

Popoluca, Walter Reuter

If I could weave, the loom is yours.
There are guitars all over Mexico.
If I could light that lamp,
The matches are yours.
There are candles in every taxi.

At every corner
The fox will sing your story:
How the child was wrapped in leaves,
Painted with a paste of corn.
A bowl in an oven. A basket
In a stream. A bus on the highway.
A blue flame.

If I could light that lamp
The loom is yours. The thread is blue—
As blue as the open sky.
Each taxi has a candle. And
With every breath of Mexico: guitars
Are weaving

For you.

ALL THINGS ARE THE NAME OF GOD

I'd forgotten. Forgot. Forgot
in need to get over our talk, the
bite. My need to get over the
hole. But I have a new *puente,* a bridge
to the next dimension. And it's
in my mouth, where the words were—

Not Spanish or Mixteca, the truth
is now, but something that my father said
when I was eight years old
that still finds its way into all-night
buses, the back-routes near León, a woman
walking with the elk
who graze the roadside in the dark

And I don't know if he spoke this
out loud or not. For it may be about
the lack of teeth—the thoughts, for
instance, that come to the deaf, the sound
of a marsh beginning to sleep
when the wading birds
have moved into the cattails

And the old men from the village
are deep inside the evening with
its bottles and their memories: what
it was like before the televisions
and the pressure cookers
and the meters on the buildings

When youths were small enough to hide
in the colors of these birds and whistle,
as their fathers did, a kind of mindless
calling, as their fathers called—to push
them into what can only
grasp from breeze and pictures

A transience like a smoke-signal
that reaches back
behind the first insistence
to make oneself
clear—as if you knew
what you were going to say, all along,
from the moment you heard it.

NOTES

ACKNOWLEDGMENTS

Grateful acknowledgment is made to the editors of the following journals in which these poems first appeared:

Beloit Poetry Journal—
"Celebración De La Carretera," "Las Hijas Del Brujo," "Triangle," "Al Río Jataté," "Shoes," "El Cervantino,"—(also the photo "Al Río Jataté")

Chokecherries—
"The Curandera And Her Son," "When Mozart Plays In Ocotlán"

5AM—
"Burros Outside San Ysidro"

Margie: The American Journal of Poetry—"Ipenema," "El Trompetista"

Nimrod—
"El Cañaveral," "La Sombra," "Woman With Pots"

Northwest Review—
"Greyfall," "Heron," "It Was Only By Chance," "Last Supper," "Los Hilos, La Tela," "Two Girls Guarding A Table," "The Dress," "Vendedora De Carne"—(with eight photos)

Poetry East—
"La Semilla," "I Weighed My Life"

Runes—
"Pomegranate"—(also the photo "Una Mirada Del Futuro")

Studio (Canada)—
"The Net," "1001 Nights," "La Anunciación," "Mujer Sembrada"—(with four photos)

Sulphur River Literary Review—"La Distrofia," "Camaleón"

Texas Review—
"Nuestra Señora De La Soledad," "Ceremonia De La Cometa," "All Things Are The Name Of God"

The Texas Observer—
"Lame Horse," "View Of Guanajuato"

Tusculum Review—
"Los Conocimientos," "The Shaman's Wife, With Birds," "Celia," Strut Your Stuff"—(with four photos)

SPECIAL THANKS

To Barry and Joan Norris, Marietta Bernstorff and Antonio Turok, Marta Turok, Pedro Meyer, Susan Dorf, Ken Nelson, Gilberto Chen, Kiki Suarez, Francisco Reyes Palma, Sandra Berler and Diana Anhalt for their help in contacting the photographers, publishers and trustees of the included photos;

To Marta Zarak, Hely Reuter, and the Fundación Mariana Yampolsky for their generous support in this project;

To Cathy Strisik, Jennifer Clement, Harlan Flint, Lise Goett, John Brandi, Lisken VP Dus, our San Miguel poetry group, for nurturing, backing this adventure from inception to bloom.

And to the photographers, for their hearts, their vision and their magic.

THE PHOTOGRAPHERS

Jonathan D. Amith
Jonathan is an anthropologist and linguist as well as a photographer, has taught at Penn and Yale Universities. He lived for five years in the Náhautl-speaking communities of Guerrero, where he has coordinated (and taught at) the Yale Náhautl Summer Language Institute since founding the program in 1998. He was instrumental, with the photographer José Ángel Rodríguez, in putting together a photo-documentary that saved Guerrero's Balsas River from a massive hydro-electric project. He has published a book of writing and photos: *The Amate Tradition: Invention and Dissent in Mexican Art.*

Ruth D. Lechuga
Ruth celebrated the indigenous face and popular arts of Mexico throughout her life. Arriving as a child in1939 from Austria, she became not only a citizen, but also an ardent devotee and collector of folk art. For four decades she photographed the culture of rural Mexico, the people and their handiwork, her work can be found in many books. Until her passing in 2004, she was director of the Ruth D. Lechuga Museum, in Mexico City.

Micaela McGuirk
Micaela was born in Los Angeles, California. She moved to Mexico City in 1975, shortly afterwards became a resident of Chiapas, where she lived and worked for the rest of her life. She devoted her last decade to the camera, and to a masterful series of photographs of the Selva Lacandona rain forest, its people and their children. She died of a brain aneurysm, following childbirth, in 1991. She was 39.

Walter Reuter
One of Mexico's most revered and beloved masters of photography. Originally from Germany, he fled the Nazis in 1939 (via the Spanish Civil War, fellow photojournalist and friend of David Capra) for a new home and citizenship in Mexico. Where he spent over six decades as a photographer, journalist, and celebrated cinematographer—his preferred theme always the life and customs of his country's *indigenas*. In 1998, he was given the distinguished "Mirror of Light" award by the Biennial of Photojournalism. He passed away in 2005, just short of his100th birthday.

José Ángel Rodríguez

José was born in Peñón Blanco, Durango in 1954, spent several years assisting Mañuel Alvarez Bravo in Mexico City. For the last four decades his realm has been that of the native cultures of Mexico and Central America, his work known for its powerful sense of the soul. His portraits of people and their personal landscapes have been published in many collections, among them his own *Vidas Ceremoniales, Imágenes de Chiapas,* and *Refugiados Guatemaltecos*. He, his wife Monique Beaudoin and daughter Sara presently divide their time between San Cristóbal, Chiapas, and Sudbury, Ontario.

Clare Brett Smith

Clare has spent her life as an ethnologist, journalist, photographer, devotee and sponsor of indigenous peoples, their arts. Her photographs—from Mexico, China, Pakistan, Somalia and countless other places—have been published in many journals, seen in numerous one-person exhibitions. Since 1951 she and her husband, Burges Smith, have lived in Farmington, Connecticut, where she serves as President of Aid to Artisans, a non-profit organization dedicated to creating economic opportunities for craftspeople around the world.

Antonio Turok

Antonio Turok is recognized as one of the foremost and compelling photographers in contemporary Mexico. Born in 1955, in Mexico City, his base for the last 35 years has been in Chiapas and Oaxaca. He has photographed extensively throughout southern Mexico, Central America—and the *barrios* of the United States. Both of his books—an earlier volume of photos from Nicaragua, and his 1998 collection from Chiapas, *El Fin de Silencio* (*The End of Silence*)—have been internationally acclaimed. He is the recipient of a Guggenheim Fellowship and the 1994 Mother Jones Award for Documentary Photography. He currently lives with his companion Marietta Bernstorff in Oaxaca.

Mark Turok

The father of Antonio Turok, Mark Turok moved from the United States in 1950 to Mexico City. Already a respected photographer, he set up a commercial offset-lithography press specializing in the reproduction of photography. Litográfica Turmex has grown to be among Mexico's most prestigious. He was known for his ability to create striking photos without the presence of the human figure—his concerns were often the compositional properties of color, landscape, and architecture, their larger human reference. He died in 2002.

Mariana Yampolsky

Mariana emigrated to Mexico City from Chicago in 1944 at the age of 21. For five decades, until her death in early 2002, she was one of the moving forces in contemporary Mexican fine art. A prolific painter and graphic artist (posters, lithographs, design, illustrations, films, publisher and author of children's books), she was also an activist, curator, and popularizer, believing that the arts were essential to public culture and welfare. But it was her work with a camera that engaged her most. From her first one-person show in 1960 to her numerous collections in books and on-going exhibitions, she was, and is still, recognized for her striking pictures of the people and architecture of Mexico.

SOME NOTES ABOUT THE SPANISH

It's hoped that these poems will be enjoyed whether the reader speaks Spanish or not. Obviously, understanding the words adds extra fun. Many of the Spanish words, such as *fiesta, jícama, celebración* and *ceremonia* are already common or kindred to English. Here are some translations of those less accessible that might be helpful:

Una Mirada al Futuro—a view of the future

PART ONE

la carretera—the road
ermitas—hermits (female), reclusives
Oxchuc—a village in central Chiapas
la selva—forest, jungle
Selva Lacandona—the Lacandón Rainforest, in southern Chiapas bordering Guatemala, homeland to the Maya
el trompetista—trumpet player
a **cantadora**—a woman singer
conocimientos—a marvelous word that can mean either "acquaintances" or, more largely, "knowledge"

106

la sombra—the shadow
la alfarera—potter, ceramicist
the **Amusgos** (and **Popoluca**)—both peoples of the interior
la herradura—horseshoe
el cañaveral—sugar-cane field
No tire basuras en la carretera—Don't throw trash on the road.
mole (*mó-le*)—a thick varietal sauce made from spices and chiles, central to regional cooking; a dish served with this sauce
camarones (*ca-ma-ró-nes*)—shrimp

PART TWO

la semilla—the seed.
la distrofia—dystrophy
las Varas means rods or rulers—as in measurement, or authority; i.e., 'the authorities.' Also the spears with which picadors torment a bull.
vendedora de carne—a market woman who sells meat
Zinacatán and **Ixcán**—both villages in southern Chiapas

PART THREE

A **curandera**—a healer, a woman who works through spiritual agency, often employing the power of **hierbas, raices**—herbs and roots
el Río **Jataté**—flows from northern Chiapas to the Lacondón border
echando redes—throwing nets
camaléon—chameleon
epazote (*e-pa-zó-te*)—a pungent culinary herb, often found growing as a weed
espinaca del diablo—Spinach of the Devil
plancha—a flat stovetop grill
cazuelas—earthenware casseroles
brujo—shaman, sorcerer
pato al horno—a turkey by an oven
Calle Limones—Street of the lemons
ollas—pots
hermánas Galán—the Galán sisters
cocos—coconuts
Nuestra Señora De La Soledad—Our Lady Of Solitude
La Anunciación—The Annunciation.
abarrotes—groceries, grocery store

El Cervantino—a festival held each year in the mining city of Guanajuato, named for Miguel Cervantes (who once supposedly lived there).

carga, cargadores—goods (cargo), loaders/handlers

A Dios!—to God

cometa—used for both a "comet" and a "kite

papaloteando—kite-flying

mujer sembrada—literally, "sown woman"

arrullo—a lullaby

comal (*co-mál*)—a shallow bowl-shaped grill, used especially to make tortillas

flores—flowers

chapulines (pronounced *cha-pu-lí-nes*)—are grasshoppers. Served roasted and salted as a delicacy in the city of Oaxaca. Brought to the plazas by people from surrounding villages such as **Ocotlán.**

Come! (*Có-me!*)—the imperative: "Eat!"

Saltar! (*Sal-tár*)—also an imperative: "Jump!"

los hilos, la tela—the threads, the cloth

el puente—bridge (over water, also of teeth)

www.ingramcontent.com/pod-product-compliance
Lightning Source LLC
Chambersburg PA
CBHW042048030726
47599CB00019B/2405